Communicating with Others

by Stuart Schwartz and Craig Conley

Content Consultant:
Robert J. Miller, Ph.D.
Associate Professor
Mankato State University

C A P S T O N E
H IGH / L OW B OOKS
an imprint of Capstone Press

C A P S T O N E   P R E S S

818 North Willow Street• Mankato, MN 56001
http://www.capstone-press.com

Library of Congress Cataloging-in-Publication Data
Schwartz, Stuart, 1945-
    Communicating with others/by Stuart Schwartz and Craig Conley.
    p. cm. -- (Job skills)
    Includes bibliographical references and index.
    Summary: Suggests ways to communicate more effectively on the job through
listening, asking questions, and demonstrating respect for others.
    ISBN 1-56065-716-2
    1. Communication in organizations--Juvenile literature. 2. Interpersonal
communication--Juvenile literature. [1. Communication. 2. Interpersonal
communication.] I. Conley, Craig, 1965- . II. Title. III. Series: Schwartz, Stuart,
1945- Job skills.
HD30.3.S3727 1998
650.1'3--dc21   97-52336
                                                                        CIP
                                                                         AC

Photo credits:
All photos by Dede Smith Photography

Table of Contents

Chapter 1

Communication on the Job

Communication is important in all parts of life. Communication is the sharing of facts and ideas. Good communication takes certain skills. Workers can learn these skills.

Workers share important facts and ideas at work. Secretaries type letters. Sales clerks talk with customers. A customer is a person who buys goods or services. Teachers give lessons and answer questions.

Employers want to hire workers who have good communication skills. An employer is a person or company that hires and pays workers. Workers must show that they can communicate well. They must be able to read, write, and speak clearly. They must be able to listen and follow directions.

Workers with good communication skills understand what their employers want them to do. They can tell their employers about problems and make suggestions. Good communication skills help people become good workers.

Workers share facts and ideas by communicating.

Chapter 2

Being Honest

Good communicators are honest. Honest workers tell the truth. They admit mistakes and talk about problems.

A cashier might give a customer the wrong change. The customer starts to leave the store with the wrong change. The cashier catches the customer and explains the mistake. The cashier gives the customer the correct change. This is an example of honest communication.

Good communicators are more than honest. They are helpful, too. For example, one cook in a restaurant might work very quickly. Another cook is a good worker but works slowly. The faster cook does not complain about how slow the other cook is. Instead, the faster cook shares ideas with the other cook. These ideas help the other cook work more quickly.

Good communicators are honest and helpful.

Chapter 3

Writing and Speaking Clearly

Workers communicate by writing and speaking. Good communicators write and speak clearly. Other workers understand what good communicators write or say.

Many jobs require workers to write. For example, truck drivers keep records of the goods they haul. They also write down how far they travel each day.

Doctors write instructions that explain how to treat sick people. Nurses must be able to read the instructions.

Teachers give lessons. They must explain the lessons clearly so students will understand.

Good communicators speak loudly enough for others to hear. They say what they mean. They ask questions to make sure that other people understand. They know that communicating is a big part of their job.

Good communicators speak clearly on the job.

Chapter | 4

Explaining Jobs

Good communicators can explain jobs to others. They can show others how to do a job properly.

For example, many workers at a factory may do the same job. New workers may not know how to do the job. Good communicators can help the new workers learn the job.

Good communicators explain each step of a job to new workers. They let the new workers practice each step. They show the new workers how to improve. They ask if new workers have any questions. Good communicators answer questions clearly and honestly.

New workers must communicate, too. They must be sure they understand how to do their jobs. Good communication prevents problems on the job.

A good communicator explains each step of a job.

Chapter 5

Listening

Good communicators are good listeners. Listening helps workers understand each other. Good listeners let each other finish speaking. They give each person a chance to speak. They think about the ideas they hear. They learn things by listening.

Good listeners show others they are interested. They look at speakers. They give their full attention. They show that they understand. They might nod their heads or answer the speakers' questions.

Good listeners often do a better job. For example, construction workers build streets and buildings. Good construction workers listen to each other. They listen to their supervisors. They consider suggestions about how to make buildings stronger and safer. Then they use good suggestions to improve their work.

Good listeners look at speakers.

Chapter 6

Asking Questions

Good communicators know when to ask questions. They ask questions when they do not understand something. But they wait for speakers to finish talking. Then they ask questions that will help them get information they need.

For example, a supervisor might tell a worker to plant 12 rose bushes. The worker could plant the bushes in one row of 12. Or the worker could plant them in two rows of six. The worker needs more information to do the job properly.

The worker asks the supervisor how to plant the rose bushes. The supervisor explains that the worker must plant the rose bushes in one row of 12.

The worker was a good communicator. The worker listened to the supervisor. Then the worker asked an important question.

Good communicators ask questions.

Chapter 7

Following Rules and Directions

All employers have rules. Good communicators understand and follow the rules. For example, food workers know their employers' rules about washing their hands. They also know why washing their hands is important.

Sometimes workers do not understand rules. Good communicators ask questions. For example, a worker might ask why work starts at seven in the morning. A supervisor explains that many orders must be sent out by nine in the morning. The worker used communication skills to understand a rule.

Good communicators listen carefully to directions. Directions are the steps needed to do a job. Following directions helps workers avoid making mistakes. Good communicators ask questions if they do not understand directions.

Bakers must follow directions. The bread may not taste good if the bakers do not follow directions. Bakers who follow directions bake good bread.

Good communicators listen carefully to directions.

Chapter 8

Sharing Feelings

People often communicate to share feelings. Sharing feelings can be important at work. For example, a team of carpenters might feel nervous about a big job. They can share their feelings. They can talk about other times they felt nervous. They can promise to help each other finish the job. Communicating helps them feel better.

Good communicators share both good and bad feelings. Sometimes workers feel angry. They might think another worker is being unfair. It helps to talk about those feelings. Workers can avoid fights by talking about their feelings. Then they can work together to solve the problem.

Sharing feelings can help many workers solve problems. For example, a teacher has to teach more students. Having more students will make the job harder. The teacher feels angry. But the teacher asks the school principal for help. Then the teacher and the principal work together to solve the problem.

Sharing feelings can be important at work.

Chapter | 9

Being Assertive

Good communicators need to be assertive. Assertive means willing to communicate thoughts, ideas, and needs. Assertive workers are often happier than other workers.

Assertive workers speak with respect. They do not yell at people when they have a problem. Instead, they try to solve the problem. They talk calmly to other workers about the problem.

For example, a secretary might run out of paper. This happens often, and the secretary has to stop working each time. The secretary asks a supervisor to place larger orders for paper. The secretary explains how this will solve the paper problem. The supervisor agrees. The secretary has been assertive.

Sometimes being assertive means questioning a decision. For example, a warehouse supervisor asks a worker to fill 80 orders per day. There is only enough time to fill 60 orders. The worker explains the problem to the supervisor. The supervisor sets a different goal. The worker has used communication skills to be assertive.

Assertive workers speak with respect.

Chapter 10

Understanding Others

Good communicators know that each worker is different. Workers come from different backgrounds. They have different knowledge and different ways of thinking. They may have different strengths and weaknesses.

Good communicators consider people's differences. They use communication skills to help people understand each other. Workers who understand each other can usually work well together.

Imagining how others feel is a good communication skill. This skill is called empathy. Empathy helps workers understand each other.

For example, a cook has trouble keeping up with orders during a busy night. The servers are upset. They do not like having to wait for the orders.

Servers who have empathy will understand. They will imagine being the cook. They will know how it feels to be very busy. They may offer to help the cook prepare the orders.

Good communicators consider people's differences.

Chapter ┤ 11

Cooperating with Others

Cooperation is working together to do a good job. Work gets done properly when people cooperate. Cooperating lets workers become part of a team. Cooperating lets them communicate their needs and their skills. Cooperating prevents fights and mistakes.

Good communicators learn about their co-workers. They learn what their co-workers' skills are. They learn about their co-workers' interests. This helps them know how to cooperate with co-workers.

For example, two doctors might get to know each other at work. They learn that they both have knowledge about a certain illness. They decide to cooperate and share their knowledge when treating patients with that illness.

Workers who cooperate care about their co-workers. They do extra work if one co-worker falls behind. They help the worker learn to work faster. Workers who cooperate know they are members of a team. They try to do what is best for the team.

Good communicators cooperate with co-workers.

Chapter 12

Communication Skills and You

Employers hire workers who communicate well. All workers need communication skills. But nobody is a perfect communicator. Some people have trouble writing or speaking. Others have trouble listening or following directions.

You can improve your communication skills. Many schools offer classes in public speaking. Colleges offer classes to help people improve their writing skills.

You can practice many communication skills on your own. If you have trouble speaking clearly, practice speaking clearly to your family and friends. You can practice writing by writing letters.

You can also improve your skills on the job. Think about how you can be honest and assertive. Listen carefully and ask questions when you do not understand. Look for ways to cooperate with other workers. Improving your communication skills will make you a more successful worker.

All workers need communication skills.

Words to Know

assertive (uh-SUHR-tiv)—willing to communicate thoughts, ideas, and needs

communication (cuh-myoo-nih-CAY-shuhn)—the sharing of facts and ideas

cooperation (coh-op-uh-RAY-shuhn)—working together to do a good job

customer (KUHSS-tuh-mur)—a person who buys goods or services

empathy (EM-puh-thee)—imagining how others feel

supervisor (SOO-pur-vye-zur)—a person in charge of workers

To Learn More

Aliki. *Communication*. New York: Greenwillow Books, 1993.

Olderman, Raymond. *10 Minute Guide to Business Communication*. New York: MacMillan General Reference, 1997.

Schwartz, Stuart and Craig Conley. *Working as a Team*. Mankato, Minn.: Capstone High/Low Books, 1998.

Useful Addresses

Canada WorkInfoNet
Room 2161
Asticou Training Centre
241 Boulevard Cite des Jeunes
Hull, Quebec K1A 0M7
Canada

Employment and Training Administration
200 Constitution Avenue NW
Room N-4700
Washington, DC 20210

Training Information Source, Inc.
1424 South Clayton Street
Suite 200
Denver, CO 80210

Internet Sites

America's Job Bank
http://www.ajb.dni.us/

Career Web
http://www.cweb.com/

CareerSearch
http://learningedge.sympatico.ca/careersearch

Skills Most in Demand by Employers
http://www.utoronto.ca/career/skills.htm

The Training Information Source
http://www.training-info.com/

Index